Gents

Toothpaste

Grape
Shampoo

# Someone Used My Toothbrush!

## * and Other Bathroom Poems *

by **Carol Diggory Shields**       illustrated by **Paul Meisel**

DUTTON CHILDREN'S BOOKS * An imprint of Penguin Group (USA) Inc.

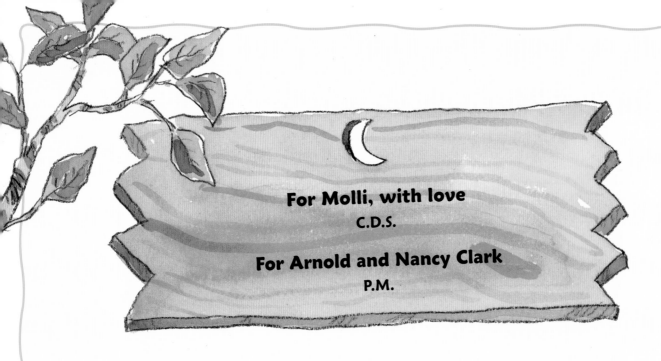

**For Molli, with love**
C.D.S.

**For Arnold and Nancy Clark**
P.M.

DUTTON CHILDREN'S BOOKS
*a division of Penguin Young Readers Group*

Published by the Penguin Group

Penguin Group (USA) Inc., 375 Hudson Street, New York, New York 10014, U.S.A. ✳ Penguin Group (Canada), 90 Eglinton Avenue East, Suite 700, Toronto, Ontario M4P 2Y3, Canada (a division of Pearson Penguin Canada Inc.) ✳ Penguin Books Ltd, 80 Strand, London WC2R 0RL, England ✳ Penguin Group Ireland, 25 St Stephen's Green, Dublin 2, Ireland (a division of Penguin Books Ltd) ✳ Penguin Group (Australia), 250 Camberwell Road, Camberwell, Victoria 3124, Australia (a division of Pearson Australia Group Pty Ltd) ✳ Penguin Books India Pvt Ltd, 11 Community Centre, Panchsheel Park, New Delhi—110 017, India ✳ Penguin Group (NZ), 67 Apollo Drive, Rosedale, North Shore 0632, New Zealand (a division of Pearson New Zealand Ltd) ✳ Penguin Books (South Africa) (Pty) Ltd, 24 Sturdee Avenue, Rosebank, Johannesburg 2196, South Africa ✳ Penguin Books Ltd, Registered Offices: 80 Strand, London WC2R 0RL, England

CIP Data is available.

Published in the United States by Dutton Children's Books, a division of Penguin Young Readers Group
345 Hudson Street, New York, New York 10014 ✳ www.penguin.com/youngreaders

*Designed by Jason Henry*

Manufactured in China ✳ First Edition
ISBN: 978-0-525-47937-6
1 3 5 7 9 10 2 6 4 2

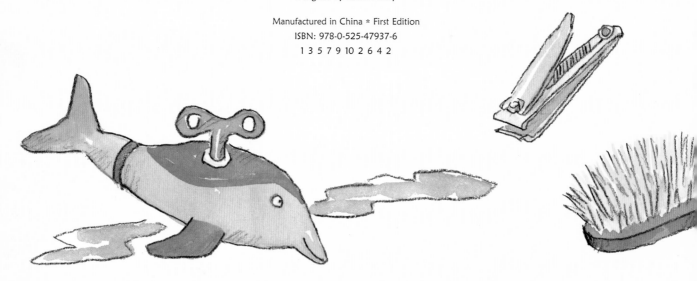

# Contents

Where to Go — 4
Soaked 1 — 6
Soaked 2 — 7
Brushing — 8
Troubles — 10
Drip — 11
Chore — 12
Waiting — 13
The Medicine Cabinet — 14
Pretty — 16
Bellowing in the Bathroom — 17
Toy — 18
Toothbrush — 20
Rush to Flush — 21
Ahoy — 22
Peace — 24
Riddle — 26
Hamper — 28
My Sister's in the Bathroom — 29
Zip — 30
Going, Going, Gone — 32

Gents

Privy

Ladies

# WHERE TO GO

Some people go to the restroom
(though it doesn't have chairs or a bed).
Other folks go to the potty.
On a boat, you go to the head.

It's sometimes called the powder room.
Some go to the Ladies or Gents.
You use a privy or outhouse
When you're camping out in tents.

It's the washroom, the john, the lavatory,
The can, the throne room, latrine.
In Spain, if you ask for the *baño*
They'll know just what you mean.

In England you go to the loo,
Or sometimes the WC.
Whatever it's called, when you gotta go,
It's the place you're happy to see.

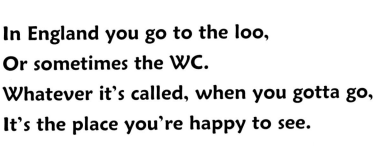

# SOAKED 1

We're soaking wet from head to toe,
Towels wet and drippy.
Suds are sliding down the wall.
The floor is slick and slippy.

The drain is all clogged up with hair.
The curtain's in a muddle.
The dog we washed just ran outside—
To jump into a puddle.

# SOAKED 2

We're soaked and scratched from toe to head.
The towels are in strips.
Footprints run straight up the wall.
The shower curtain's ripped.

Fur is flying through the air,
And we are swearing that
We will never, ever again,
Try to bathe a cat.

# BRUSHING

Oh I'm glad I'm not a crocodile,
'Cause brushing my teeth would take a while.
I'd go to bed late and get up early,
Just to keep my teeth all shiny and pearly.

I'm glad I'm not a hippopotamus.
I'd have to use an enormous brush
And tons of toothpaste, in a great pile,
To scrub, scrub, scrub my hippo smile.

I'm glad I'm not a great white shark,
Brushing my teeth, alone in the dark.
I might look in the mirror late at night
And give myself a terrible fright.

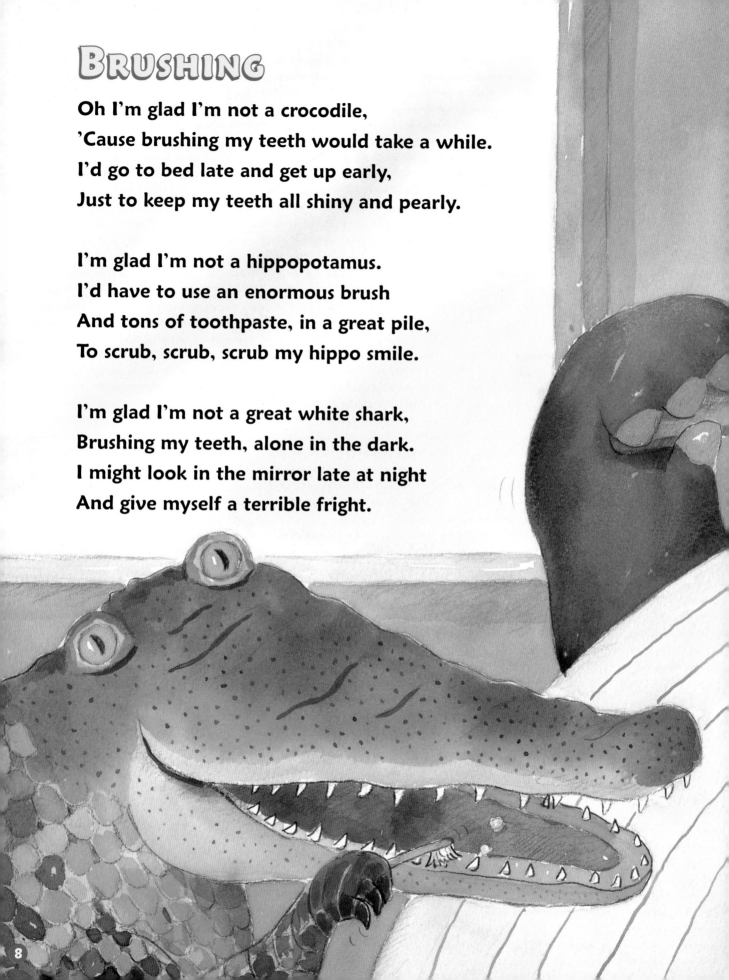

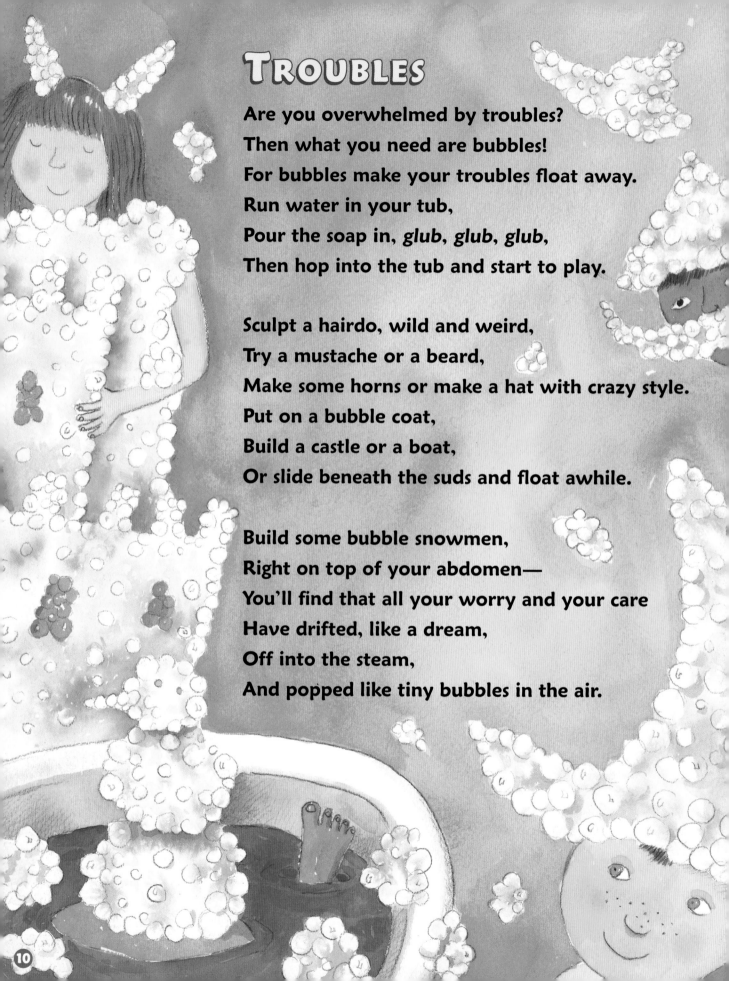

# TROUBLES

Are you overwhelmed by troubles?
Then what you need are bubbles!
For bubbles make your troubles float away.
Run water in your tub,
Pour the soap in, *glub*, *glub*, *glub*,
Then hop into the tub and start to play.

Sculpt a hairdo, wild and weird,
Try a mustache or a beard,
Make some horns or make a hat with crazy style.
Put on a bubble coat,
Build a castle or a boat,
Or slide beneath the suds and float awhile.

Build some bubble snowmen,
Right on top of your abdomen—
You'll find that all your worry and your care
Have drifted, like a dream,
Off into the steam,
And popped like tiny bubbles in the air.

# DRIP

The bathroom sink, the bathroom sink,
All night long goes plop and plink.
A *drip*. . . a pause. . . and then a *drop*,
Like torture that will never stop.
I twist the handles, turn them tight,
But still from dusk till broad daylight,
Sleeplessly, I flip and flop,
While the sink repeats. . .
plip. . . and. . .

plop.

# CHORE

This chore is ucky,
Gross and mucky.
When it's my turn
I say, "Oh yucky!"

It smells all musty.
It's kind of crusty,
Damp and dank,
And even rusty.

It's the chore
We all abhor,
Cleaning the toilet,
Where it meets the floor.

# WAITING

We've offered treats and sweets and toys,
Said, "Pretty, pretty, please."
Demonstrated how it's done,
Begged and praised and teased.

We've squatted nearby patiently,
For minutes, hours, days.
Read books out loud, sang silly songs,
Put on puppet plays.

We've cheered and scolded, babbled on.
We're slowly going dotty.
But we have faith—somehow, sometime,
The baby *will* go potty.

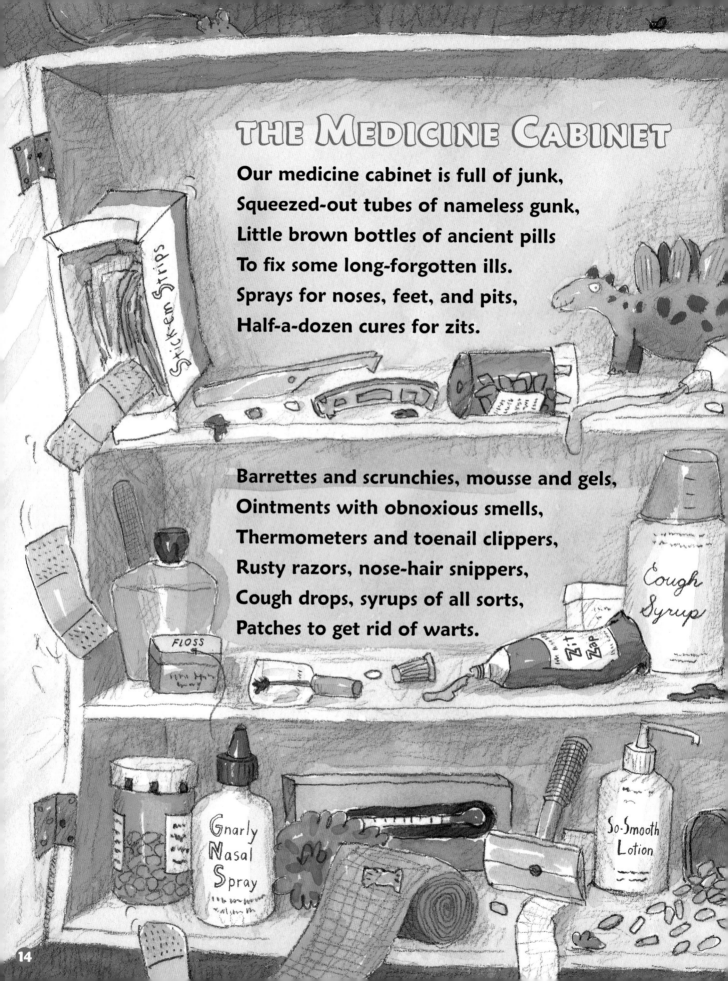

# THE MEDICINE CABINET

Our medicine cabinet is full of junk,
Squeezed-out tubes of nameless gunk,
Little brown bottles of ancient pills
To fix some long-forgotten ills.
Sprays for noses, feet, and pits,
Half-a-dozen cures for zits.

Barrettes and scrunchies, mousse and gels,
Ointments with obnoxious smells,
Thermometers and toenail clippers,
Rusty razors, nose-hair snippers,
Cough drops, syrups of all sorts,
Patches to get rid of warts.

Wipes and swipes and salve for sores,
Two small plastic dinosaurs,
Sunblock, sunscreen, sunburn lotions,
Tiny jars of mystery potions,
Bandages and dental floss,
Fake tattoos and old lip gloss.

Safety pins and dye for hair—
Open up that door with care,
For if you don't, then you will chance
A medicine cabinet avalanche.

# PRETTY

Jen's busy in the bathroom,
While Mom is on the phone.
Jen is wearing jewelry,
High heels, and cologne.
Her lips are red, her cheeks
  bright pink.
Her eyes are blue and green,
Purple, orange, and yellow,
And some colors in between.
Jen thinks she looks as pretty
As a lady on TV.
But Jen looks pretty funny,
Since she is only three.

# BELLOWING IN THE BATHROOM

There's a bellowing in the bathroom
Like a mad moose on the loose
Or perhaps it is a rhino,
Or a loudly honking goose.
Could it be a wounded bison?
A gorilla's mating call?
It bounces off the ceiling,
And echoes down the hall.
Could it be a brontosaurus
Roaring at full power?
No, it's just our dear old dad,
Singing in the shower.

# TOY

The baby's found a brand-new toy,
A never ending source of joy.
He tugs and pulls, it rolls and twirls,
And swoops about in flowing curls.
He waves it, throws it here and there,
Puts it on, like long white hair.
Baby giggles in delight.
It seems there is no end in sight.
He drapes the tub, the cabinet door,
Covers every inch of floor,
Stuffs it in the brimming bowl—
He's found the toilet paper roll.

# TOOTHBRUSH

Someone used my toothbrush.
That isn't very fair.
Someone used my toothbrush.
Dad said we shouldn't share.

Someone used my toothbrush.
They thought I couldn't tell,
But it's soggy, kind of greenish,
And it has a funny smell.

My sister said, "Just use it!"
But I don't think I wanna.
I think she used my toothbrush
To scrub our pet iguana.

# Rush to Flush

Tell me why this happens—
When I am in a rush,
The toilet picks that moment
To decide it will not flush.

I jiggle and I joggle,
But the water's hesitating.
Outside the door folks gather.
Everyone is waiting.

The tank is slowly filling,
No faster than a trickle.
Someone's yelling, "Hurry up!"
Now I'm in a pickle.

I pump the handle up and down,
Then suddenly—oh no!
With a mighty rush of water,
It begins to o
      v
       e
        r
         f
        l
         o
          w.

# AHOY

We're all brave mates aboard this ship,
Setting off on a dangerous trip.
We'll face tall waves and crashing seas
As we sail about the Island of Knees.
On the Good Ship Sponge we'll meet typhoons,
Wind-up sharks, and pouring monsoons.
We'll need to be swift, fearless, and plucky,
If we're attacked by the Big Yellow Ducky.

Past towering cliffs, so far from home,
Fighting off pirates through billows of foam.
Ho for the sailor's life, wild and free,
Exploring the boundless Bathtub Sea.

# PEACE

"I need some relief! Twenty minutes of peace!"
Mama slammed the bathroom door.
We all felt bad for Mama,
So we thought, and thought some more.
Poor Mama, we sighed, in the bath by herself,
She must feel so alone.
Then Ryan had a good idea
And found Dad's old trombone.

Amy got the pots and pans,
Wooden spoons and tins.
Jennifer got out her guitar,
Gave rattles to the twins.
Then we sang some songs for Mama,
Though the words didn't always rhyme.
When Mama came out she was laughing—
And she cried at the very same time.

# RIDDLE

It sits in the bathroom,
Looks quite ordinary,
Yet we tiptoe around it,
Like it's very scary.
When Dad's in there with it,
He gives out a groan.
Sis sometimes screams,
And Mom starts to moan.

Brother ignores it,
Says "What's the big fuss?"
And Grandma—well, who knew
That Grandma could cuss?
And yet we all use it,
Though fear turns us pale—
That one-eyed monster...
The bathroom scale.

# HAMPER

My shirt is in the hamper,
The one I need to wear.
I put it in a week ago,
And it's still sitting there.
I burrow through a mountain
Of towels, socks, and shorts,
Everybody's underwear,
And uniforms for sports.
I find it near the bottom,
Where it's been squished and
  squashed.
I figure—it's been there so
  long,
It's just like it's been washed.

# MY SISTER'S IN THE BATHROOM

My sister's in the bathroom—
What does she do in there?
How long can someone floss their teeth,
Or comb and brush their hair?

My sister's in the bathroom—
Is she napping in the tub?
If you need to go real badly,
Go outside and find a shrub.

My sister's in the bathroom—
You can knock and plead and call.
Or you can join the rest of us,
The line forms in the hall.

# ZIP

Zip! Zoop! Off it goes,
Slithering across my toes.
I leap and grab it, hold it tight.
It takes off like a bird in flight,
Lands and rebounds off the taps,
Does a couple high-speed laps,

Around the bottom of the tub—
I capture it and try to scrub.
But like a squiggly, squirmy fish,
It zooms off with a soapy swish.
They say light's fast, but I say nope—
There's nothing like the speed of soap.

# GOING, GOING, GONE

"Go before we leave the house,"
Said my mom and dad.
But I forgot and didn't go—
I really wish I had.

'Cause now I'm in the backseat,
We're on an endless road,
And I gotta go so badly,
I think I will explode.

I'm hanging out the window.
My teeth are tightly clenched.
We have to stop, we have to stop,
Before my pants get drenched.

At last we find a restroom,
(Just before I burst).
Now I know, when you're going to go,
Make sure that you've GONE first.